I'm Reading About

OREGON

The Beaver State!

GALLOPADE

by Carole Marsh

Printed and Manufactured in Peachtree City, GA., USA
www.gallopade.com

Book design: John Hanson

Editorial manager: Janice Baker

Oregon is a great state.

It is one of a kind.

What makes Oregon special?

Let's read about it and see!

NATIVE AMERICANS

Who lived in Oregon first?

Native Americans did!

They moved around to find food.
They hunted in Oregon's woods.
They fished in Oregon's rivers.
They gathered fruits and seeds and nuts.

EXPLORERS

Some of the first explorers to Oregon arrived in 1778.
They came from the country of Great Britain.

Captain James Cook was their leader.
He and his men landed at Cape Foulweather.

SETTLEMENT

Fort Astoria was the first permanent settlement in Oregon.
It was built at the entrance to the Columbia River.
Fort Astoria was a trading post to trade animal furs.

Many of the furs traded at the fort were from beavers, sea otters, squirrels, and red foxes.

Fort Astoria
Fort Astoria

STATEHOOD

Oregon was the 33rd state
to join the United States of America!

Isn't it great,
to be a state!
I bet Oregon
could hardly wait!

Oregon became a state in 1859.

Oregon
The 33rd State
Here we are!

FLAG

I am the state flag.
I was adopted in 1925.

What color am I?
I am blue.

Look at me.
What else do you see?

I fly high over the state of Oregon!

STATE OF OREGON
THE UNION
1859

CAPITAL

Say hello to Salem,
the capital city of Oregon!

There is an important building in Salem.
It is the State Capitol.
Oregon's laws are made there!

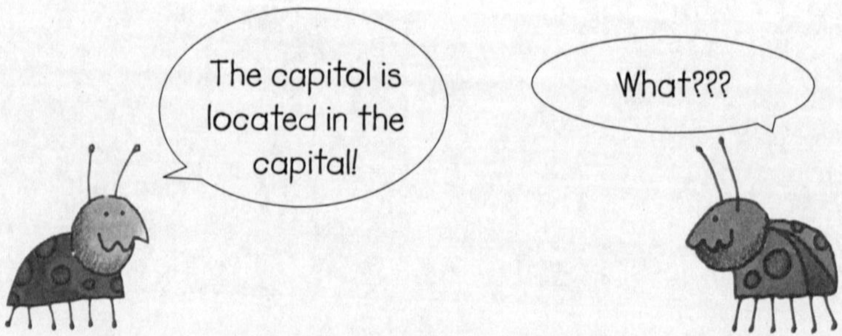

Capitol

SEAL

I am a seal,
but I am not the State Seal.
If I were, I would be very important.
I would be stamped on many official papers.
(Ouch, that might hurt!)

STATE OF OREGON
THE UNION
1859
Now, that's official!

NICKNAME

State nicknames are fun!
State nicknames are great!
They share fun facts
about each state!

Oregon's nickname is "The Beaver State."

Beavers are smart and hard workers.
They are just like people from Oregon!

The Beaver State
OREGON
welcomes you
My nickname is "The Red Bug."

BORDERS

Look at Oregon.
Oregon is in a region called "the Northwest."

Oregon borders four other states.
Find them on the map!

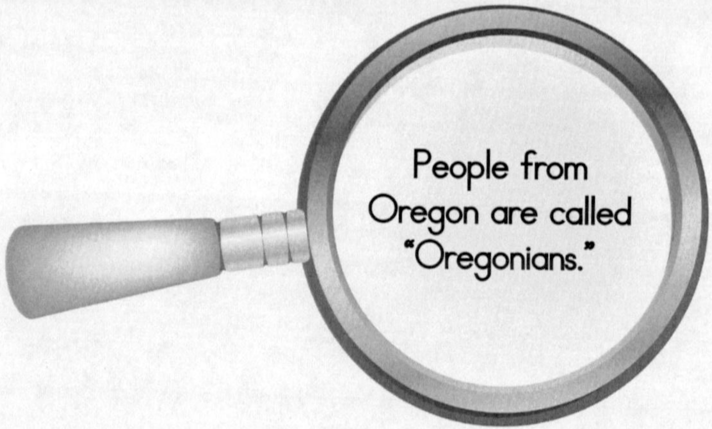

Borders

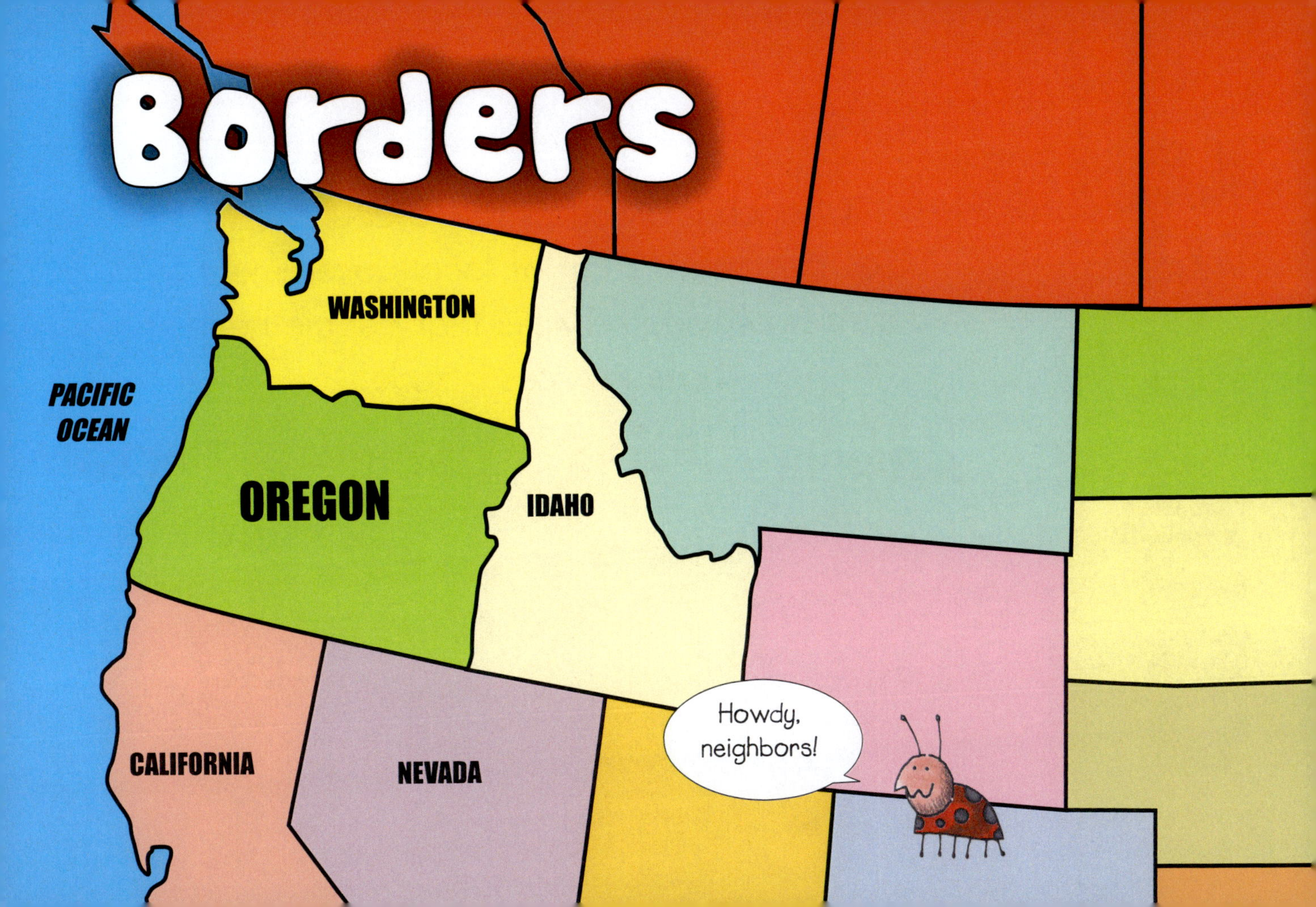
PACIFIC OCEAN
WASHINGTON
OREGON
IDAHO
CALIFORNIA
NEVADA
Howdy, neighbors!

COUNTIES

Oregon is divided into 36 counties.
Counties are a form of local government.
Counties provide services that people need!
Those services include:

Schools **Parks** **Libraries** **Police**

Firefighters **and More!**

Counties

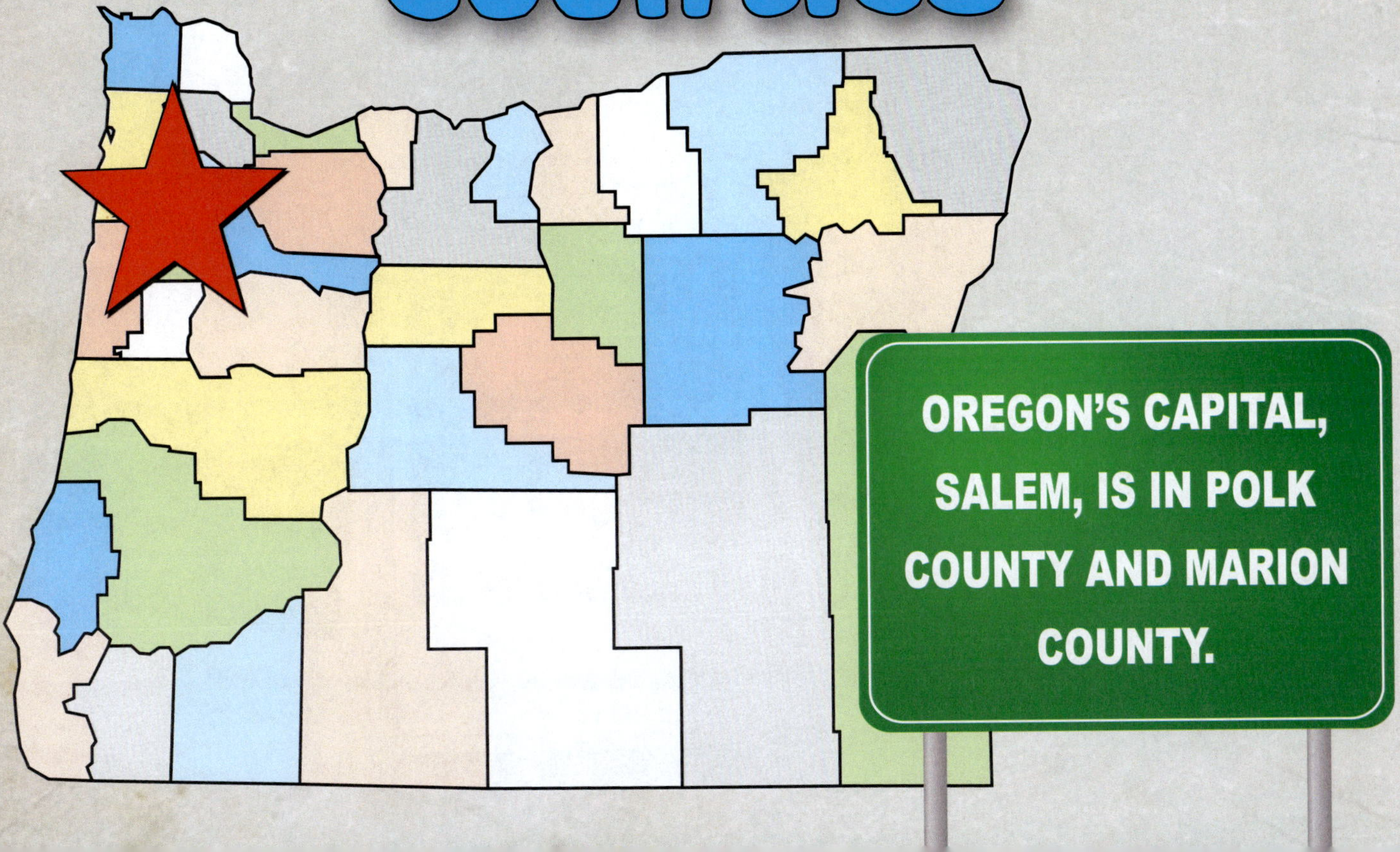

PEOPLE

Many famous people

Chief Joseph
Nez Perce
Native American leader

Bill Bowerman
Track and field coach who co-founded Nike, Inc.

Douglas Engelbart
Engineer who invented the computer mouse

call our state home!

Barbara Roberts

Oregon's first woman governor

Dick Fosbury

Olympic athlete who invented the "back-first" technique for high jump competitors

Matt Groening

Cartoonist who co-created *The Simpsons* television show

PEOPLE

Western Meadowlark

BIRD

I am the state bird, and I fly
over Oregon, proud and high.

As I fly, up in the sky,
I flap my wings to tell you "Hi!"

The Oregon state bird is the Western Meadowlark.

Oregon Grape

FLOWER

I am the Oregon Grape.
I am the state flower.

I grow where it's warm and sunny.
I bloom in early spring.
I help make Oregon beautiful!

Look at me! Smell me!
I grow dark blue berries in the fall.

Douglas Fir

TREE

I am a Douglas Fir—I'm the state tree.
All over Oregon is where to find me.

My roots run deep, they keep me strong.
My leaves stay green, all year long.

I stand up straight, big and tall.
Don't climb too high—it would hurt to fall!

Oregon Swallowtail

INSECT

I am the Oregon Swallowtail.
I am the state insect.

I flit and I fly from flower to flower.
I am looking for nectar to drink.

Look at my beautiful wings.
What colors do you see?

Pacific Ocean

Let's go to the beach!

We can swim in the waves.
We can play in the sand.

We can build a big castle
where water meets land.

Oregon's beaches are home to many animals:

Fish **Seals** **Birds** **Crabs** **Dolphins** **and More!**

BEACHES

Cascade Mountains

MOUNTAINS

Oregon's Cascade Mountains are the place to be.
Hiking, fishing, camping—
fun for you and me.

Winter weather brings lots of snow.
Temperatures drop to freezing and below!

Forests

FORESTS

Oregon has many miles of forests.
The trees are tall.
Their leaves are green.
They cover hills and the valleys in between!

This habitat is home to many animals:

Deer **Bobcats** **and More!**
Hummingbirds **Bears** **Bald Eagles**

Almost half of Oregon is covered with forests!

Crater Lake

Hey! I can see my reflection in the water.
You sure are funny-looking!

LANDMARK

Crater Lake is the deepest lake in the United States!
It was formed when a volcano erupted.
The eruption left a deep crater
in the top of a mountain.
Rain and melted snow filled the crater with water!

Crater Lake's water is crystal
clear and bright blue!

Oregon Crops

AGRICULTURE

Oregon has many farms.
Why?
Because Oregon has good soil and a mild climate!

Some of the top crops grown in Oregon are:

Hazelnuts **Hay** **Wheat** **Potatoes**

Hey!
Don't forget about me!
Oregon farmers raise lots of cattle, too.
Moooooooo!

Sports in Oregon

SPORTS

Baseball! Basketball! Football!
Oregon has it all.

Whether you like to watch or play,
You are sure to have a ball!

Trail Blazers

Timbers

Beavers

Ducks

& More!

Oregon: Home of Timber

CLAIM TO FAME

Oregon is known for its timber!
Timber is wood used for building and carpentry.
Oregon produces the most timber
in the United States!

Many of Oregon's trees are also used to make paper.

GLOSSARY

carpentry: making or repairing things with wood

cartoonist: a person who creates cartoons

climate: weather conditions in an area over a long period of time

crater: a large bowl-shaped hole

erupt: when a volcano explodes with lava and ash

habitat: a place where plants or animals naturally live

laws: rules made by the government

nectar: a sweet liquid produced by plants, especially flowers

region: an area that has similar characteristics

settlement: the first community in an area